Colonial Pipeline Hack

Colonial Pipeline Hack

The CEO of the Colonial Pipeline came to a difficult conclusion that on the evening of May 7th — he had to pay the $4 million ransom to the overseas hacking group known as Darkside; a decision I can assure you was not on his agenda when he had ended the workday on the 6th.

That morning the 7th, an employee found a hacker's ransom note on a control room computer. IT and Security teams sprang into action, but inadequate endpoint protections had the virus fully entrenched within the systems of the Colonial pipeline. By nightfall, the full severity of the situation was starting to sink in.

Oversight by the IT Team and/or insufficient cybersecurity has given hackers access to a VPN account from an employee who is no longer employed. VPN usernames and passwords were available for sale on the open dark web.

The Colonial Pipeline has over 900 employees and provides 45% of the fuel to the east coast. The bulk of their equipment consists of pipes and tanks that stretch thousands upon thousands of miles, all without computers. With our increasing reliance on the efficiency computers bring to the business, the cyber attacker found a weakness. The values used to turn the pipes on and off and the sensors used to measure flow and quality control all run on computers. These computers feed data to the company systems, so without this information, the company cannot operate.

The company spent lots of money on IT support

each year, but it wasn't enough, and the result was headlined on the news with lines for gas on the main street. In 2021, cyber-attacks have been rampant, leading to many high-profile headlines.

The first half of 2021 had multiple high-profile breaches.

- Jan 2021 - Microsoft Exchange Zero-Day vulnerability
- Jan 2021 - Solar Winds compromise, which had 25% of all businesses compromised.
- Feb 2021 - VA breach compromising the personal data of over 25 million veterans.
- March 2021 - Adobe Flash Player Zero-Day vulnerability that was present in 900 different software packages.

- May 2021 - NDTV hack compromised 800 million accounts just by clicking on a link from an email

In all these cases, there were multiple layers of security and many would assume they are safe but as we can see, that is rarely the case! These high-profile cases are dwarfed by the huge number of small and medium businesses being hit daily.

No one knows when they will become the next victim of an attack. Cybersecurity attacks happen more often than you might think — over 85% of organizations have been attacked at some point in their history and nearly 60% have had data breaches within the last year alone. The last 12 months have seen more cybersecurity breaches than the previous 15 years combined!

For many cybercriminals, small businesses are a low-hanging fruit. They're easy to find, and they often have poor IT infrastructure with many vulnerabilities, which means a breach can be fatal for the business.

History of Cyber Crime:

Hacking is changing the way a product or procedure functions. When you use a butter knife to open a can of paint, you are "hacking". The term was first credited with use in 1960s when model train enthusiasts at MIT modified their trains for fun.

These curious individuals went on to work with early computer systems where their curiosity led them to discover how internal coding was done.

Some of their hacks became so successful that they outlived the original product. UNIX, developed as a hack by Dennis Ritchie and Keith Thompson, is a notorious example. To the general public though, “hack” simply means an ingenious way to fix or improve something quickly.

"Hacking" became a household term in 1970s. When early computerized phone systems were first deployed, hackers discovered that certain tones and numbers would result in free long-distance service for them. They impersonated operators, dug through garbage cans to find secrets from Bell Telephone Company, and tested how to exploit a system by "cracking" its secrets.

In 1986, Clifford J. Stoll became aware of irregularities in data at the Lawrence Berkeley National Laboratory and crafted a honeypot tactic (a tempting pot of data) to capture an unknown unauthorized user who was hacking into his network. The intruder turned out to be Markus Hess who had been selling information to the Soviet KGB. The rise of the nation's state-sponsored cyber-attacks has begun.

In 1988, Robert Morris (who happened to be the son of an NSA employee) created the most destructive Internet virus yet, known as the "Morris worm". This thought exercise was just to "see if it could be done" and ended up infecting close to 10% of the internet. The virus successfully infected an astonishing 6,000 computers.

A coding mistake in his file, which had the virus reproduce itself regardless if it already existed on the computer, resulted in the first Denial of Service attack and crashed many of the systems it was found on by continually reproducing itself until the hard drive (computer memory) was full.

Father of Ransomware:

The first credited ransomware virus was created in 1989 by Harvard-trained evolutionary biologist Joseph L. Popp called the AIDS Trojan. It was distributed as 20,000 infected diskettes labeled "AIDS Information – Introductory Diskettes" to attendees of the World Health Organization's international AIDS conference in Stockholm.

The disks, when inserted into a computer, would run a program that purported to do nothing more than display information about the disease. The program, however, contained code that would encrypt the users' data and instruct them to send $189 to a PO box in Panama for the decryption key.

Numerous attacks between 1989 and 2008 were attempted with varying levels of success. Locking the user's files was easy, and the difficulty came with large-scale payments without getting arrested.

When Bitcoin emerged in 2008, it was a game-changer for ransomware. The decentralized cryptocurrency provided a new, mostly anonymous system for collecting funds – making it much more difficult to trace payments.

Hackers now have a proven method of attack with a newfound method for collecting payments discretely.

2013 was a turning point for cybersecurity because of the Cryptolocker release. Cryptolocker is estimated to have infected around 250,000 systems and generated over $3 million for its creators.

Despite being a relatively new threat, ransomware has already become one of the most damaging forms of cybercrime. Between 2013 and 2021, ransomware attacks skyrocketed as these criminal enterprises got more experienced and sophisticated in their attack methods.

What do cybercriminals want with your small business?

Hackers don't care about your small business, right? Wrong! If you have money they would like to have it. Like the pirates of the Caribbean Sea in the age of the sail, modern internet pirates seek defenseless merchants loaded with treasure traversing the digital oceans of our planet.

These seas are one no business can avoid. We call these pirates Cyberterrorists, Hackers, or Cybercriminals, but a rose by any other name is still a rose. They want your treasure.

The hackers will create many unique ways of convincing you to part with your hard-earned money. They'll try to trick you into revealing personal information like passwords, credit card numbers, and banking information. They might also steal your company's trade secrets or send malware that can delete all the data on your computer.

How do we protect ourselves against hackers? There are three key ways: education, prevention, and protection. Reading this book is likely a sign that you are interested in getting educated about cybersecurity for your business. With cyber attacks on businesses skyrocketing every year, it is more important than ever to work on preventing your business from being hacked.

We will dive more into prevention and protection later in this book.

Say hello to your friendly neighbourhood hacker:

Data analysts often describe hackers as younger people seeking quick and easy opportunities to make a considerable profit or gain fame. They are driven by greed, boredom, or the desire for notoriety. They have no regard for the consequences of their actions and they'll stop at nothing to achieve their motives regardless of law enforcement actions. Unlike other criminal activities like drugs, human trafficking, bank robberies, or prostitution, cybercrime is not geographically restricted.

Hackers can sit at a beach in Florida one morning, then fly to Spain the next without ever losing track of their activities. Imagine being a law enforcement agency trying to track hackers who have little more than a string of numbers as to their location.

Our example hackers were two IT professionals who worked for a call center that provides IT support to restaurants throughout North America and Europe. They lost their jobs when the company was shut down in April 2020 due to Covid.

Hackers' Plan:

The two hackers devise a plan to go after the customers of their previous firm: they are performing this attack through "phishing" credentials from the company's email database.

They used their previous contacts at the old call center to send fake email blasts to restaurants for password reset requests. The attempt had the end-user verify their password which gives the hackers the original password.

This email blast resulted in capturing passwords from 150 end-users out of the 20,000 users that were targeted.

Reviewing the email accounts that were compromised, they found that 30 of those accounts had invoices in the sent mailbox.

These clever hackers craft a message like the one below and resend the invoice requests, but add urgency to the request and a big discount if the invoice recipient acts. "<Company Name>, in an effort to expedite collection of the funds, if you will wire money to 12345-4837422 bank account by 5 pm tonight, we will give you a 20% discount off the attached invoice."

It's a simple but effective phishing scam that pays off for the young group.

Meet your small business owner Bill

Bill's Furniture Company has been in business for 35 years and started out in the garage. The company is now flourishing with twenty employees, serving upper-end builders of homes and restaurants.

In his office, Bill has two computers; one for communications with clients (his laptop) and another he uses for his bookkeeping.

Hackers and Bill connect.

One of Bill's clients was in a group of 30 that were compromised by hackers. These hackers sent a new email from the compromised account, which included an attachment to Bill's bookkeeper which was very common, so she opened it.

Unknown at this time was that the hacker, not the client, sent the email and attachment. At this time, the attachment has a remote access trojan, custom written to avoid anti-virus detection. The hackers have remote access to Bill's accountant's computer and sit quietly on the computer to start learning the behavior.

These hackers spend a few days watching, getting familiar with the computer systems and where critical data is kept; in other words, creating a project plan for how to attack.

The remote surveillance allows them to discover that Bill's IT team had set up an automated backup of the accounting data and files. A review of the bookkeeping email shows that MUCH larger invoices are sent out from Bill's account than previous targets. This justifies a multi-prong attack.

1. They reconfigure the data backup to exclude the accounting folder but keep the data backup going. A spot check of the backups will show they are still working. Then wait 1 month for the backed-up data to drift.
2. 1 month later, they attacked with ransomware on all computers and servers.
3. Simultaneously, they performed an invoice email scam on all clients last month.
4. After successful ransomware, they send a request to the IT team to remote into the computer because of the virus. This remote action allows a virus to be uploaded into the IT company's computer systems if they are not using zero trust endpoint protection.

Bill is in trouble at this point and the above attack is not "the perfect blend of an unlucky guy". This is a normal ransomware attack from an experienced hacker. It is why 1 in 5 businesses that are hit with a full server ransomware attack go out of business. His IT guys are great guys, but IT and Cyber Security are very different and it is important to understand those differences.

Your business was just hacked, now what?

If you just got hacked, this is not the book for you. You are looking for guidance on how to get unhacked; this is a book we wrote specifically for business owners on how to protect themselves from being hacked and ransomed or make a compromise of little value to the hackers.

Let's pretend for a moment that you did. If your IT company is unable to get your data back, then get a new one immediately. To date, not a single client of mine that has taken our managed and cyber-security options has ever lost data from a cyber attack. We have a healthy sense of paranoia and a motto of "Trust nothing, verify everything".

If you have a good resource to help navigate these waters with you, then it is time to pull up the backup disaster recovery (BDR) plan. You should take an assessment of what data you have and how much of your data has been lost.

It's a good BDR plan and you can tell those hackers to shove their ransom right up their....... computers.

If this assessment proves a less happy outcome, in that the hackers were able to successfully deny you access to critical business data that you have located in no other place, then it's time to evaluate if you can or should "pay the ransom".

This is risky but not as bad as you might think. It is often cheaper to pay the ransom than to lose the data. In 2018, the City of Atlanta had a ransomware attack and ended up paying more on lost revenue than the ransom!

A subcontracted accountant for Atlanta had access to the Accounting Server that was hit with ransomware, similar to what you can see in our previous chapter example. The hacker realized that the data they had access to from their accountant was worth much more than just the ransom demand.

The hackers gained access to Atlanta's systems through the accountant's credentials and edited the back-ups for their accounting system to exclude accounting files and waiting months. They then attacked again, ransomware their server.

The city chose not to negotiate with terrorists and they were able to avoid paying a $52k ransom. This cost the city over $2.6 million in lost revenue, all from cyber intrusions.

Paying the ransom does not guarantee that your files will be decrypted or restored. If you pay the ransom, there is an 80% chance that you will get your data back. 4 out of 5 are not great odds, but it's better than none. A good disaster and recovery plan with cyber protection has much better odds!

I can't afford to protect my business.

Like TV ads for stray cats or orphan donations, for less than 50 cents per day, you can protect your employee from a cyber attack! Company owners need to be aware of the risks, but operating without competent cyber protection leaves your business more vulnerable than if you have no insurance.

You would never dream of running your business without the essential coverage to protect against such catastrophes as fire, workers' compensation, and auto insurance. The risks are too high! One accident away from ending your business. Yet, more businesses are likely to have ransomware attacks this year than they are to have a fire in the next decade!

A properly protected computer (aka endpoint) can be done for as low as $12.50/mo. The average cost to employers of an employee per year is about $50k/year, protecting their computer from such huge threats are pennies on the dollar!

That may be a bit tongue in cheek, but the message is clear: it does not take much to prevent cybercrime and ransomware from wreaking havoc on your business.

I will address this more in a later chapter but if you only read this chapter, I want to make sure this point is known. The anti-virus and AI-driven antivirus programs are not cyber protected as I will explain in later chapters.

My IT guy/girl/firm handles cyber protection for me.

I hope you have a sound cybersecurity plan, because if you rely solely on your IT person, then they will largely be dependent on their own knowledge.

There is no 3rd party certification or validation in our field of IT / Cyber Security. Accountants have a CPA license to uphold, a lawyer has a bar, and electricians have a state board. IT and Cyber Security have nothing.

We happen to be the smartest person in a room on IT and get thrust upon us the expectation that we also know how to fight cyber criminals and nation-state actors from a system compromise.

Our field has some GREAT IT firms/girls/guys that never wanted to know anything about cybersecurity. They wanted to fix people's computers and that's it.

They know how to install the applications that they are told to install. Being good with computers does not grant that person a magical knowledge of all things tech and how to fight off every known compromise. That is like telling a CNA that he/she should know how to do heart surgery because they are in the "medical" field. Someone in the "tech" field does not know how to do all things tech.

I can't tell you if your IT firm is doing a great job for you or if they are the victims of their own success and serving you up as a tasty lamb to the slaughter of hackers. Here are a few things I would like to ask myself.

5 questions to ask yourself to find out if you have the right IT firm.

- Have they implemented a Zero Trust endpoint protection policy on all devices?
- Are they passionate about multi-factor authentication for all of your devices?
- Do you know if your backup data has been revised? If not, you're susceptible to ransomware and other cyber-crimes. Perform a test: Delete an important file from the server, and set a reminder in Microsoft Outlook for two months later. If they can't get the data back, then your backup is bad.
- Are they testing your employees for phishing attacks?
- One last point to consider is whether they are attending 2-3 in-person cybersecurity events a year and coming back with education on the latest attacks. If they are the smartest

person in the room, does he or she seek out the larger rooms with smarter people to learn from?

A list like that above gets two responses depending on who I'm talking to.

Scenario one: You're a business owner who has used the same tech for years, your kids go to the same school and they coach your basketball team. Perhaps you have someone in-house who has been with the company for a long time, knows your system inside and out, and has many other critical job functions as well. It can be hard to tell them that they are falling behind on cyber protection.

If you find yourself in these situations, contact a CoMIT IT Firm with a focus on Cyber Security. CoMit (Co-Managed IT) works with in-house teams and outside teams who handle IT and supplement their abilities. Ask for a free security assessment to be performed and tell the firm you want to have the IT items to stay with your current resources. In my industry, this is very common.

Your in-house IT staff and long-time business associates might be great at setting up your computers and printers, but these days, it may be worth bringing in a third party with expertise to help ensure you're moving forward in the right way.

Scenario two is that you are an expert in cybersecurity. If you look at my list and want to know things like:

- Blacklisting of IPs from known compromised sources like North Korea or Russia
- Check server logs to identify errors and login attempts
- Password and password restoration policy
- Review VPN logs for potential intrusions
- 100 other checkpoints that are all important

However, this book is written for business owners on how to protect themselves from cybercrimes and ransomware. This chapter specifically is written to help business owners who don't know how to review whitelisted IP addresses and how they can measure their current IT support.

Most business owners don't know how to check for those and would need to ask their tech for that info. The questions are designed to allow a non-technical business owner to know if he/she is being asked the correct questions by their techs and if not, take action to preserve the relationship with their current resource while getting the protection they need.

Maybe you are an IT and are afraid for your job. You can work with a company to make sure that your network stays secure without having to give up your duties. CoMIT (Co-Managed IT) firms are great at protecting companies against all sorts of cyber threats while working with current IT resources. These firms will work with you, not against you.

Waiting until a major security breach occurs before taking action and getting the help you need from experts is not going to save your job. Let's be proactive in our approach.

A good CoMIT work with you, have tough conversations with your boss and/or owner about what they need to do and why, and leave the tech work to you. This also gives you the resources you don't have in case you ever get stuck or want to deploy a new solution.

My boss does not value cybersecurity

You value your position and would like to continue in it for a while. As you read this book, it has become abundantly clear that you're not well prepared for a cyber attack.

As you address these points with your business owner, he/she says a line similar to "I have been in business for ___ year and we have never had a ransomware attack....." and the conversation ends there.

I've heard that result, or a similar response to it, many times. It's similar to going back to 1950s and telling people, "Smoking will kill you," and they respond with, "Grandfather smoked 10 packs a day." Today, we know that smoking kills. However, there are a few who have managed to live long lives while doing it.

Cyber threats as a business killer are new within the last 3 - 6 years on such a large scale. The time will come when your owner wants to take it seriously. It is hard to want to spend a very limited resource of money on something they don't see as a real threat.

What can you do...

- See what type of IT budget you can get for Data Backup and Disaster Recovery, and then work with a firm that can à la carte a protection plan for you. If you can't get a budget to stay protected, make sure you have a good backup strategy so when you are attacked, you can recover.

- Become knowledgeable on the types of backups and see if you can be an advocate for better and stronger forms that have protection from ransomware.
- If a breach occurs (email compromised, password leaked, a critical business file goes missing), bring that to his/her attention and ask them to look at options to prevent or solve it with a reliable vendor. Do so respectfully. If you go into the boss's office with the "I told you so" attitude, expect to be ignored. Sugar gets better results than vinegar.

- Follow as many of the steps in the next section of "Steps Every Person Can Do to Start Protecting Your Business Today".

I am the founder and CEO of multiple companies and have found that it can be difficult to come around at times to new ideas my team brings to me. Remain vigilant and respectful. Be assertive about security standards, but don’t come across as a know-it-all. Use your voice to gradually raise the bar for others.

Cyber Security you can start today

It is no surprise that you would want to get right down into the meat and potatoes of this subject. However, let's stop and congratulate you for sticking it out even when all these technical terms are overwhelming!

Step 1: Assess your current team:

This is a good time to take out your list of staff members and start brainstorming on who should be on a small team of decision-makers. At my firm, we go to teams of 3 for big decisions. The team should start out discussing what is important to the company. Create a fun name for this team like "Defenders of the Digiverse" or....

I don't. It's your choice!

Step 2: Ask the team: If they had a magic wand, what would they improve about your IT infrastructure? A list of questions could include:

- Do you need more remote access?
- What security features would you want to add?
- If credentials of IT administrators were compromised, could they corrupt or delete backups? What about other users' data on the system such as emails, customer information, etc.?
- Are you leveraging any zero-trust endpoint protection tools?
- Who is managing the zero-trust endpoint for definitions of software and network traffic that is trusted?
- How often is traffic reviewed?
- When is the last time you did a full restore test of the disaster recovery system (digital fire drill)?
- When is the last security conference your team attended?
- When is the last time you reviewed your exposed credentials from a dark web search?
- What was your monthly phishing failure rate from last month? Do you even have an email compromise test?
- What is your average time to detect, analyze, and remediate an intrusion?

- Do you have a plan for how to manage when employees leave (voluntarily or involuntarily)? Do they get their laptops returned before leaving?

Step 3: Contact a professional for an assessment. Most firms offer free assessments, and the consultant's reports can indicate areas of weakness you can correct in order to protect your business from cyber-attacks and ransomware.

Working with a cybersecurity consultant is a challenging decision, especially for small business owners who want to protect their systems but are unsure of the options and prices.

Refer to the chapter "My IT handles my cyber protections", there's a list of 5 things to look for. Make sure all outside consultants you hire cover these basics. If they don't, it's time to search for someone else who can.

Similarly, if you went to a burger specialist and they didn't have ketchup, you would question if they really understand American burgers. Likewise, the 5 questions in that chapter give you an inside guide to be able to judge the competency of this new IT / Cyber Security vendor.

It’s all about finding a good business partner for you. If you can, have the owner of the firm come to the meeting.

For my firm, I like to start out with three plans after an assessment, which I call "Bullet Proof, Bullet Resistant, and target Practice" with prices ranging from $150/mo/pc to $15/mo/pc (as of 2021). If a client can't or doesn't want "Bullet Proof", we start talking budget and reverse it based on what they are looking to protect and discuss vulnerabilities as a result.

Business owners should understand their company's possibility of cyber crimes and ransomware before using any security strategy. Open dialog with an IT firm will help them come up with a plan that is right for their business.

Anti-Virus is dead

Anti-Virus is the first thing everyone thinks of when they think of cyber protection. But it's not enough. If you want to protect your business from the latest cyberattacks, AV isn't going to cut it.

AV is a reactive measure, which means that when someone releases an exploit out into the wild and it gets propagated through email attachments or websites with malware scripts, they'll release a new version of their product in order to block those threats before users get infected — usually about every two weeks on average. This doesn't mean that any company using this strategy will be safe for long though as there are many variants of ransomware being released and updated daily by hackers around the world! The bad guys know what we're doing too; anti-virus just can't keep up anymore.

This is referred to as "signature-based detection". Your anti-virus software updates with new virus signatures, the antivirus provider found. Hackers, being the smart people they are, have found ways around this.

Top 3 ways hackers can get around anti-virus:

- Write a custom virus daily: Anti-Virus needs to have found the virus. If the hacker adds a few letters or numbers to the file each time they deploy it, that virus will go right past almost any anti-virus software.
- Write a new copy of the virus when their virus is detected. Hackers have anti-virus software on their own computers. They can update the anti-virus software and if it detects their recent virus, they write a new one and deploy the new one.

- Do not use viruses, instead use stolen credentials and install industry-standard software for remote access.

The growing use of anti-virus software is a flawed approach to computer security because modern cybercriminals have developed simple ways around it.

Advanced Anti-Virus (AAV) - a step in the right direction but not enough

The next evolution in endpoint protection is the Advantaged Anti-Virus. Malware Detection and Network Protection combine the best of the two worlds. You can detect malware that manages to get past traditional anti-virus software by looking for malicious behavior in real-time on your device or network.

This AI on your PC looks for things it sees as malicious and stops them while leveraging the signature-based protection of an anti-virus. A much better defense but one critical flaw: it allows anything it doesn't see as dangerous to run.

This leaves hackers with the challenge of creating viruses that are quiet enough they don't get caught by the AI.

Another flaw is the flagging of False Positives. AI Antivirus deployments are occasionally accompanied by false positives. Backups can be disabled even when they're whitelisted, and games on personal computers could stop working if a false positive triggers the tool's analysis of it.

We even had the email server shut down once because the tool falsely flagged the core file thes being a ransomware attempt.

These false positives are better than not having the protection so we used them for many years. That is until the gold standard in protection was refined.

Zero-Trust Endpoint Protection: Antivirus and AI AntiVirus's critical flaw is in how they look at the problem. They are trying to find the needle in the haystack, scanning every file that comes into a company's network looking for things it knows are bad. This means they have no way of knowing if something is good or bad until it arrives on your PC and starts executing (or not).

Zero Trust takes an entirely different approach to cybersecurity than Antivirus does by looking at everything from the perspective of how should we treat this thing? If it's a program you know, then it goes straight through; if it's unknown, it doesn't go. Trust nothing, verify everything.

This sounds simple and you might wonder why it took so long for the computer world to get to a zero-trust standpoint. If you go to a concert, they don't scan you for "likely doesn't have a ticket". They require you to prove that you belong there or you get kicked out. This is security 101.... why did the IT industry take so long to catch up to this standard?

Computers are hard and have 1,000's of applications and files that all talk to each other. Each one gets updates from the development firm which changes its code. Zero trusts in the past would have required upkeep on all those files or would cause critical files to stop working every time the computer updated one of its subprograms.

Modern IT infrastructure has enabled us to track those changes and implement zero-trust frameworks so businesses can operate effectively and securely while accounting for software updates and new versions.

It makes it so we can improve service delivery for clients. Every client I meet has that old piece of software that requires administrative rights to run correctly. With Zero trust, we can give that program administrative rights and because the zero trust framework is controlling permissions, it results in no risks.

Microsoft Exchange Zero-Day Vulnerability Jan 2021, almost every onsite exchange server in the US had foreign hackers inside them. The hackers could install programs to ransomware, steal credentials, or elevate other permissions. All except those that had zero trust protections installed. Those servers with zero trust protections installed still had hackers gain access to them, but those hackers were locked into a vulnerability and could not use that compromise to expand their influence on the server.

In order to protect your business from cybercrime and ransomware attacks, you need Zero Trust Protection. Without it, your system is asking for it to be compromised.

Data-Backups: The Ark for your digital flood

Noah's building of the ark to create a backup of the human race and all living species is a good analogy for your backup disaster recovery (BDR) plan.

The Ark for your digital flood and data-backups is a life raft that may help you survive a disaster. Your business will have to navigate its way through floods of new technologies and changes in an ever-changing landscape, so it's important to be prepared with backups of all your files on whatever storage media makes sense for your company.

I have given 1000s client assessments and have seen every imaginable version of a data backup. They range from a USB drive that is rotated by the assistant on occasion to fully automated revised cloud backups with onsite and offsite restore capability.

What are you protecting against?

This may seem like a silly question. Obviously against the loss of your data. But as important as knowing how that data loss can happen, I want to do a thought exercise on what you are protecting against? What you are protecting against plays a lot into how elaborate of protection you need.

For example, you want to protect against a hard drive failure on your main server or a fire in the server room and your data loss tolerance is 1 or 2 months worth of data. A USB that is randomly rotated is fine if that is all you're afraid of.

If your accounting data is stored on that server, your data loss tolerance might be significantly less and require a much more elaborate system.

Description of Data Loss:

- **User Error** – If an employee deletes something from a computer by accident or alters the information, then your protection plan would need to include backup methods that hold data revision.
- **Physical Loss or Hardware Failure** - Data storage devices can fail. If your backup device fails, then you need to ensure that there are multiple copies available and stored in different locations.
- **Ransomware** – Ransomware encrypts files and lock them down, preventing users from accessing any of their

information until they pay for keys or find some other way around the ransomware and decrypt the file themselves. Protection from this includes offsite data revision (onsite data revision or even multi-site data duplication could result in all onsite backups getting locked up in the ransomware attack).

- **Data System Corruption** - Data system corruption can cause data loss. To prevent this, you need to have a backup that is separate from the corrupted one.

Since we now know what we are protecting against, let's look at the different types of data backup.

USB Drive: (also see tape drive, CD/DVD, and other removable media)

We have all done it. We have this super important document that we want to make sure is extra protected so we throw it on a random USB drive to make sure we can retrieve it. The problem with this is that USB drives can be easily lost, damaged, and corrupted.

This is a simple, cheap, and easy form of data backup that works well for one-off situations and short-term solutions.

Some cost-conscious business owners see it as working well for a one-off solution and think they can use it as a process in their business for all critical business items. The scenario goes something like this.

The company set up a rotation process for their USB drives. The goal was to provide three backups in order to minimize the risk. Everyone felt safe when this went into practice — they were not prepared, however, for the realities of life every business face.

Key employees who are responsible for information security can sometimes forget to do their job one week and neglect the task sometimes because their boss gave them a super important job to do, like prep for a meeting with a giant new client or fix a delivery issue with a super important client on the production floor. In the craziness of the week... or week(s), those items got missed.

The problem is, these key people who would be trusted with such a task do eventually get busy and don't have time to do it every week. Or they leave the company, and no one remembered that as one of their job duties.

The second huge issue with this is the data drift. When the backup plan was set up, the USB drive had all the critical data. There is a nice, automated script that runs daily, moving the files over. Scripts break but no one notices. The USB drive is getting rotated weekly like it is supposed to, then the flood comes. It's time to pull up that the backup only to find the backup files are 3 years old. No one was checking the files to make sure the backups had good data on them.

Worst yet, you might have had a hacker go in, see the script was backing things up and modifying it so it puts what looks like good files on the USB but the files are not usable. (See the story from the City of Atlanta in the chapter "Your business was just hacked, now what?").

As a backup strategy, I give this method a grade of a D. It's better than nothing but will fail you on a long enough timeline.

Offsite/Cloud Backup:

You have moved on from the rotated USB drive and have a cloud backup solution. It is safer than a USB drive because it's not sitting in your office waiting to be infected with ransomware as an employee could do accidentally or for malicious purposes, and when you have off-hours access to what should be safe backup files.

This backup solution has its downfall. The two most notable are the lack of revision and reliance on a script that can fail.

Script or software failure in a backup is very common. My team spends many hours a month fixing and repairing clients' backup systems as we monitor them. A knee-jerk reaction to solving this is to put alerting on. Send an alert when a backup doesn't take place. Sadly, if the script fails, the alerting can also fail.

Scripts fail because the computer system (Apple or Microsoft) releases an update that changes how the system works and the script no longer runs. They can also send a bad update that breaks a previously working part of the system only to fix their bad update with a good update that doesn't restart the script.

Those human-caused reasons all the way to the random electron flying through the universe from a supernova many years ago end up hitting earth and striking your computer perfectly to switch one of the 0's on your hard drive to a 1, breaking the script. I don't know why or how every computer script breaks but decades of experience tell me they do.

Lastly, ransomware. If your data is encrypted by a ransomware attack and the script is sending data to the second server or to the cloud alternative, it will replace all the good backup files with the newly encrypted ransomware files. Upon going to your backups, you will be horrified to learn they are the same ransomware files you have onsite.

The backup solution is a C, better than the USB drive but with lots of holes in protection.

Full Server Virtualization with revision and offsite

We have worked our way up the ladder of protection. This is a great solution for businesses with multiple servers and lines of business software running on them.

In this case, copy your full server's hard drive as a backup into a private bootable cloud storage area. In the event of data loss or cyber attack, you boot up the cloud server, then access it through a remote desktop from anywhere in the world at any time.

What happens if the cloud server is ransomwared? This is the beauty of revision. Let's say the hacker did get all the files on the backup server ransomwared. Look at what time it happened and restore revisions prior to that. With a revised server, every time a file is changed, it keeps the previous version as well as the new one. This allows us to restore a single file or the entire server ensuring we never lose the data.

This works for things as small as a single file that accidentally got deleted, a disgruntled employee who deleted the "super important never delete" folder from your server and a full-scale cyber attack. It is "almost" bulletproof.

What is the risk? Glad you asked! We have the same issue if the backup script is modified without knowing or the settings of the backup are modified. What happens if the backups just stop and do so for a month?

This is becoming more and more common with hackers and especially with ransomware attacks. A company owner who has no other backup copies will pay substantially more to get their data back if hackers are the only ones with a copy of it. This means hackers are trying to disrupt data backups without throwing alarms, leaving business owners with a warm, fuzzy feeling of safety until they try to restore them from backups.

Professional ransomware crime gangs will have significantly more experience editing and adjusting backups than most IT techs, so don't underestimate their experience or knowledge in this area. Some gangs will have specialists with specific types of backup systems so they know how to edit the configurations without throwing any alarms or how to continue false positives of "good backup" to notification sources.

This risk has me grade this backup strategy with a grade of B. Outside of a targeted attack, it gives a reliable backup.

Full Server Virtualization with revision and offsite with nightly disaster recovery testing and verification

Lastly, we have a solution that protects you from the flaws in the above solutions. At the time of writing this book, it was the top shelf, the gold standard of disaster backup and recovery.

The addition of a nightly disaster recovery test and verification. This will help you stay on top of any errors or issues before they can lead to a disaster. A digital "fire drill" or proof of your backup strategy can be done successfully.

The concept behind a disaster recovery test is to simulate the complete loss of the primary server and verify if the backup solution can have a usable and working server.

It has been my experience that without the "fire drill" and test of your backup, no matter how good your other backup solutions are, you're at risk for data loss.

You may be thinking that this level of protection sounds amazing but the cost is outrageous! Cost is a relative thing. If your backup was a $20 USB drive you bought 3 years ago, then any monthly service would be outrageous. If you are currently paying an employee to perform the tests weekly or monthly, the labor time alone might make this a saving.

My firm offers this style of backup for a single server with 1 terabyte of data for $197/mo and can be customized for your unique use case. It’s worth you looking in your area at what your current vendors offer for pricing and solutions.

These are the solutions I would grade at an A+

Single access to data backups, an unknown risk.

Can any single person at your company remove all the data from your server? If the answer is a yes, you are at a huge risk.

At my firm, I do not have access to all the passwords. That is because if I did, and if I was compromised, I am a HUGE liability to the company. A hacker getting my access would be a dream come true for them. We look at each team member and think, "What can we take away from them and allow them to do their job?"

You should do the same and your data backup plan should include within it "What happens if the CEO/IT Administrator/CTO gets hacked". Kevin Mitnick was giving a speech at a conference I was attending about his security firm. If you don't know about Kevin, he was on the FBI’s 10 most wanted for hacking NORAD and other firms in the '90s. During his trial, he was denied a "phone call" and denied use of the phone for years because he was feared to be able to launch nukes off through the use of just a phone.

He now has a penetration testing firm that is paid by some of the largest companies in the world to test their security measures against outside intruders. He has never had any issue getting inside of these client's networks and he continues to have a 100% success rate with gaining access to impersonate them while inside.

If your strategy for protecting yourself is that "I am the only one who has access, so it's safe", then you are in danger. Computer hackers can fool a system into thinking they're you if they have the right credentials by pretending to be you with a server.

Conclusion:

In conclusion, decide which strategy fits your company's goals and budget. Know what your risks are and how you will handle them when the day comes to put them into practice. If you are not a tech, I would recommend consulting a reputable firm that works with businesses.

Passwords without MFA are worthless

A short story on passwords. The 1st computer systems did not have usernames and passwords because it was a small group of people who knew each other. As the group grew larger, they started having "user names" and creating a password. Very simple, many just used "password" as the password.

Then came the computer security team who saw the misuse and wanted to make it more complicated. They said, "We want upper- and lower-case letters". So, they used "Password". Not pleased, the security team wanted to make it more secure and said, "I want a number as well". So, the users updated it to "Password1". Finally, they said "I need a symbol in as well" and the world responded with "Password1!".

I hope the story above does not make you want to run and change your password. For decades, security lists and dark web scans have shown surprisingly that passwords like "Password, password, passw0rd, 123456, qwerty and others" have topped the list of end-user passwords.

Most users think of passwords in terms of another human sitting at their keyboard trying to guess it. A human can guess 10 - 20 words a minute if they type fast and click log in. Chances of them guessing the exact use of your password would take some time, and you throw an ! or something at the end and, boom, you're secure!

Hackers try to work smarter, not harder. Guessing someone's password through computational methods is called "Brute Forcing". Software that is brute is forcing another system to not try 10 - 20 passwords a minute. They can try up to 1,000,000,000 a second. Billions are hard for our brain to understand, so let me give some examples:

- This list enables them to try all the top 1 billion used passwords in the world instantly.

- A dictionary containing about 500,000 words would take less than 3 minutes to try every combination of words together.
- The average person knows 35,000 words. It could try every combo of the top 35,000 known words in about one second and all combinations with numbers and symbols behind those words in a few minutes.

With all the data breaches in recent years that have resulted in the exposure of personal information such as Social Security Numbers, birth dates, and childhood friends' names, and other Personal Identifiable Information (Pii), these hackers can start having those scripts try combinations of birthdays, friends, streets you grew up on, anniversary dates and more at a rate of 1 billion a second!

I have hammered this point, so I'm sure you'll understand that humans are not at their best when it comes to selecting passwords and computers perform excellently at guessing them.

Use password savings and randomized password generators to have secure user credentials. Even this alone isn't enough to keep you safe. My firm gives every client of mine a password safe to use for free.

The most common way hackers get your password is by asking you for it, either through an email that seems to be from a trusted source or over the phone. Yes, end-users will give a hacker their password over the phone if they think it's an IT guy trying to help them.

This method makes even the most secure password able to be phished from you against your will. This is why multi-factor authentication (MFA) is a must!

MFA is a form of identification that is required when accessing your account. This could be in the form of a text message, email, or through an app on your phone.

Investing in MFA will keep you safe from any phishing attacks and other hacking methods because it requires a breach of a second form of verification, most often on a separate device like a phone or fob.

You are likely familiar with this from your bank and other systems you use. In your business, every credential you use should require an MFA token of some kind.

What do you do if the user account does not have a dedicated email or phone? FOBs can be used for this! FOB is a hardware device that you can use to control multiple accounts. They are physical devices displaying a pin code that is entered at login time and they generate their own six-digit number which changes every thirty seconds.

This makes them almost impossible to hack because there is no way to know the next sequence of numbers and it's near impossible to guess what those numbers will be when they change. This also provides peace of mind if your phone gets lost or stolen because all access stops with the loss of your physical key fob.

What's the best thing about MFA? It takes just minutes to set up, typically only requiring an email account and some other credentials from you on hand and makes hacking much more difficult. It is at its own risk and security experts are already looking at tri-factor authentication and other more secure means.

DarkWeb Scanning

No matter how safe and secure you are, eventually, your credentials will get leaked to hackers. This can happen even if you maintain perfect password hygiene in all areas of life.

We read a lot about hacks in the media and my firm runs a dark web credential scan for all the new clients I meet with (give us a call if you want one done for your company). When we run them, we often find credentials from LinkedIn, DropBox, EatStreet, and other popular services that had data breaches and hackers got the username and passwords from those sites.

The overarching concern with these breaches is that employees are using their passwords in multiple locations. Assuming my firm starts working with you and makes the employee learn one super secure password. This 8 to 12 digit code is fully randomized and would take years to crack. We feel safe and life is good.

This employee goes home and LinkedIn asks them to update their password. Do you think that employees will learn a new 12 digit code? No, they don't, they enter the one they had to use at work. They then signed up for EatStreet and a million other accounts using that password.

Hackers breach 1 of those services and then try that username and password on 1000 different sites to see if the employee uses it in multiple locations. Once they are done with it, they sell the credentials to other hackers to use.

Let's say your business has 40 employees in it and each employee uses their work password at home for social media, email, online shopping, etc... You have just created a big hole for hackers to infiltrate. Scanning the dark web for credentials that come up for auction is a huge advantage in protecting yourself from these online breaches.

Employee Phishing Testing and Training

Some employees may not be aware of the risks they are taking when it comes to phishing scams. Worse yet are the employees who think they are so smart they would never fall for a scam.

When I went to college, our professor who taught network security told us a story that had happened to him a few weeks prior. He got done teaching a class on phishing and credential theft. Went to his computer and his PayPal asked him to verify a transaction he didn't make. He clicked on the link and logged into PayPal only to realize, as he pressed enter, that the site was not PayPal. He was just phished!

At my company, a side of me loves it when our phishing tests catch our senior technical employees. We all laugh and giggle because we know that they know a million times over how to spot suspicious emails and how to look for links, these guys could teach classes on it but still get caught.

Do you think you're wrong to spot every phishing email? Employee phishing training is imperative to avoid hacks! Anyone who thinks they can identify the sophistication of modern phishing emails 100% of the time is kidding themselves.

These programs are surprisingly easy to implement. These phishing training systems send fake phishing emails designed specifically for people in different roles. Salespeople might receive a fake salesforce login or an email prompting them to reset their Office 365 account, while someone in finance might get a banking password from the system and so on.

With these programs, we find out who are the weak points of our employees and also what areas people don't understand about cybersecurity issues. We can then use that information to educate them better with other training materials as well as create more awareness around privacy protection at work.

There's an added personal touch to our phishing tests — employees who inadvertently fall for a phishing attack must complete a short 5-minute video on what happened.

This means that in the future, team members will be even more diligent about email scams when they know any failure could mean training from the tech team.

At the end of every day, when a real phishing attack happens, they are so wary that it's an IT health check, thus leaving your company safe from a breach and employees more diligent about protection.

Keep your system up to date

Install new updates and reboot your computer, or remind me later? How many times have we clicked the remind me later button? IT Techs have a love/hate relationship with system updates.

Why do they keep pushing these updates to our computers? The truth is because the software you bought is broken and still not working correctly. Software development is the equivalent of writing a million-line math program whose answer is a graphical screen. In most cases, its workability is unknowable to the human brain.

The programmer thinks he/she is telling the computer to do one thing, but it ends up doing something unintended. When sections of code start interacting with other sections of the code, unintended actions start multiplying and no amount of testing can catch them all.

So, software makers find bugs (or unintended features) and prioritize fixing them. These fixes can correct the mistakes in the original code but can also introduce additional problems.

One time, Microsoft released 3 patches for Windows 10 over the course of 3 months that had an "unintended feature" of disabling printers on devices running an accounting system, affecting about 5% of our firm's endpoints. Our clients were not pleased nor were we.

Logic might suggest uninstalling any of these patches and keeping things as they are. If it works now, why risk breaking it? And with some systems that might be true, especially if the updates are from smaller companies and do not contain security patches.

The risk of not patching computer systems is that there are always flaws in the original code. One recent example is Microsoft Exchange Server's January 2021 Zero-Day Vulnerability, but new security issues crop up constantly with no end in sight. Developers fix one only to create another unintended flaw without realizing it.

Patches will be a part of life for the foreseeable future and keeping systems patches will be required for security and protection, even if the fixes end up breaking other things.

Get your internal IT some help in Cyber Protection!

The skills, experience, and education of your internal IT team range based on your company's size and industry. Those on the internal IT team are often the unsung heroes of the company. They keep everything running and only get notices when something is not working.

In many companies, I have seen that it is almost always assumed that the IT person knows everything there is to know about computers. This is not the case.

As a small business owner, you need to know what your internal IT team does and what they do not do — so that you can be aware of any gaps in their knowledge or skills.

The problem is most business owners are under-qualified at judging the skills of their team members in tech. You know for sure they are better than you are, but when compared to the industry as a whole and/or when stood up against an experienced hacker looking to ransomware all your data and go toe to toe against everything the internal tech had to offer, how well will they match up?

In most cases, my experience with internal IT teams is that they score very highly at making sure the data is protected against physical loss such as fire or theft, but not against a hacker.

They are highly skilled at PC setup and understanding how to configure the computers for the users.

They know the ins and outs of how the server and software run.

Review the chapter on "My IT handles cyber protection for me". In it, I give you some questions to ask yourself on how good of a job your internal team is doing.

If they score badly, that does not mean they are bad. You hired them to be a tech, not a cybersecurity specialist. Let me really hit home on this.

- When was the last time you offered them a $5,000 budget to go to a 3-4 day cybersecurity conference and let them rub shoulders with industry experts? That is the cost of attending most of these types of conferences and I attend 4 - 5 of them a year.

- Do you require them to meet with local firms to stay up to date on product offerings?
- Are they given budgets to test out software that they might be interested in applying to your company?

The single biggest question to ask is if you want the new hire to be your primary cybersecurity specialist. If they are, make sure they have adequate tools to succeed in their job; this can get expensive quickly. Alternatively, consider partnering with a local cybersecurity company that can offer guidance and assistance for specific tasks.

What to look for in a Cyber Security / CoMIT / MSP

You met internally and decided you needed to bring in some help to get a second opinion on your network.

Start with the end in mind. First, you want to identify any special certifications you need. The banking industry needs SOC-2 compliance, my firm works with a lot of medical and manufacturing companies, so we maintain HIPAA validation and comply with ITAR/NIST security. Identify what compliance requirements you must start reviewing.

Time to find a vendor. Ask other businesses who they use and share with them a few of the questions in the "My IT handles cyber protection" to see if their IT does cyber protection.

Next, call their phone number. My advice is, if you get an answer by number routing system or thrown into a voice mail, move on.

If they start your experience out without a live answer from someone, it is likely going to go downhill from that point. I have heard stats as high as 80% of IT firms do not answer the phone with a live person and send you to the voice mail graveyard.

Meet with them and look for the points discussed in the "My IT handles cyber protection". Ask about services, contract lengths, and guarantees. Here are a few points I must watch out for.

Contract Lengths: In our industry, clients are often pitched a 1, 3, or 5 year contract length to be able to work with an IT provider. Try to get as short of a term as possible.

These vendors will cite things like "We put a lot of work in on the front side of the contract and need to make sure you stay". Or some version of this story. The truth is, every vendor puts in work when they get a new client, especially in IT.

We need to document your network, create and understand user profiles, deploy backup and disaster recovery, review onsite hardware... and a huge list of other items.

You should strive to work with a vendor whose service delivery and customer service alone will keep you with them for 5, 10, or 20 years without the need for a contract forcing you to stay and allowing you to grow or shrink as your business needs dictate.

Guarantees: Do they have any? An example of a few items my firm offers:

- We answer 99.3% of all calls with a live person.
- Of the 0.7% of calls that go to voice mail, we will pay $100 when that phone call is

not returned within 60 minutes during business hours.

- We don't mark up any of our hardware, you get it for the price we pay.
- If you are not satisfied with our work, we want a chance to make it right. If we can't fix the problem, then let us know and we will step away from the job for you.
- Signing up for our team is month-to-month, with no long-term commitments.

These are a few things to keep in mind as you compare providers for your company; make sure you create a checklist for the different assurances from the firms that sound important.

Pricing: Find a firm that will work with the budget you have.

At the end of the day, you should want to work with a business partner that is going to support you as your company grows. A good business partner will also help guide you through these murky waters and help turn them into a pure freshwater stream you can confidently drink from.

Conclusion:

Good luck on your journey into the world of IT Support and Cyber Security. Every year in the last decade has seen double- or triple-digit growth in cybercrime from the previous year.

As we look to the future, this number will grow. Currently, around 50% of the world has access to the internet, leaving billions of people without access. Internet access is seen by some as a basic human right and huge pushes are being made to bring the last 50% online.

This is a cause we should all champion as those of us who have access to weather, internet how-to videos, and medical diagnosis sites take it for granted. Everyone should have this access and the poorest people of the world currently do not.

Efforts like Starlink from SpaceX are the leading contender to bring this access to the last 50% as soon as this year 2021. This will have unintended consequences we in the business world need to understand.

The last 50% are also the poorest people in the world in areas of instability from a government perspective, offering perfect breeding grounds for cybercriminal organizations to set up shops.

Now is the time to start hardening our defenses for your data!

About Rod Holum Jr

The CEO/President of Coulee Tech, Inc. is a leading provider of cyber security protection, IT Support, and Software Development; specializing in Healthcare and Manufacturing clients in Wisconsin, Minnesota, and Iowa; headquartered out of La Crosse, WI.

Rod Holum has been featured on the Fortune 5000 Fastest-Growing Private Companies in 2019 with 900% growth over a 3 year period and again in 2020.

When he's not kicking off the butt of cyber criminals, defeating slow computer networks, or writing amazing software solutions, he enjoys hanging with his wife and family in their back yard by the pond, investing in the youth group boys at First Free (shout out to his 10th Grade Men! #Boaz2036!), or having his Cyber Security & IT Rockstar team over for the grilling of some meat products and beverages.

The greatest joy of his life is his wife of 20 years, Laura Holum, who you may glimpse while playing keyboard at weekend services for First Free Church, and his amazing 3 kids.

Aspen(14) His mini clone, attends Aquinas High School and just got her first job at Features in Holmen! Side note, she is happier than she looks in the picture.

Jeremiah(12) His son who is Rod's #1 video game companion and co-pwner of noobs online. Jer (as he's called) also dabbles in coding amazing solutions in his Arduino kit.

Ezra(10) His youngest whose smiley happy personality is contagious to all she is around. She enjoys dreaming about horses and playing barbies.

www.ingramcontent.com/pod-product-compliance
Lightning Source LLC
Chambersburg PA
CBHW071256050326
40690CB00011B/2423
* 9 7 9 8 5 1 7 9 9 4 8 3 7 *